2019

Unquiet Energy

Alex Mowbray

Chris — THANK YOU!
You and yr team have challenged, empowered & blessed in all you have brought. Refresh will be different now — it cannot be the same.
So, may you know peace and energising, the beauty of love and the healing power of Truth.
I'm sure we'll meet again .....

Alex & Evie

night.parables@gmail.com   07855 344584

Unquiet Energy

Onwards and Upwards Publishers
Berkeley House, 11 Nightingale Crescent, Leatherhead, Surrey, KT24 6PD.
www.onwardsandupwards.org

Copyright © Alex Mowbray 2012

The right of Alex Mowbray to be identified as the author of this work has been asserted by the author in accordance with the Copyright, Designs and Patents Act 1988.

All rights reserved.

No part of this publication may be reproduced or transmitted in any form or by any means, electronic or mechanical, including photocopy, recording or any information storage and retrieval system, without permission in writing from the author or publisher.

Printed in the UK.

ISBN: 978-1-907509-67-4

Cover illustration: Alex Mowbray
Graphic design: Guilherme Gustavo Condeixa

Other illustrations:
p9: Nicole Matthews
p27/45: Ruth Griffin
p71/83: Alex Mowbray

Contents

Introduction 5

Journey 9

Beauty 27

Mortality 45

Hope 71

Purpose 83

To Evie and Hannah whose love and support is constant and to my parents who have taught me so much – their labours have not been in vain.

It is my hope and prayer that all who read these pages will be encouraged on their earthly journey to discover all their Creator has for them and live in the hope of Heaven.

Alex Mowbray

Introduction

He was quiet as I leaned over and put on his seat belt. He would always wear a belt however short the journey – a man of routine whether making tea for Mum using her favourite bone china set (complete with Hermesetas) or trimming a pink fabric plaster on his permanently cracked thumbs.

I would smile at this attention to detail – he knew I thought he was fussy, but he would call it being particular. He asserted that Mum was worth it, and they were the only thumbs he was going to get. He would chuckle as he reminded me that I one day would be his age and I too would have routines that my children would laugh at.

My Dad was invariably cautious, a 'what if' man who could be tiresome at times – he would always consider the risks and leave little to chance. He never liked car parks; he would drive round and round a multi-story in search of an end space with plenty of door room. Once he took twenty seven minutes to find the right position, and even that was a compromise. I could have done all my shopping in that time but it would have been cruel to abandon him.

Dad was the child of a war generation – instinctively careful with money yet always generous. Sometimes when I stop for petrol I remember his weekly pilgrimage to the local Jet garage several miles from home to save a few pennies per gallon. I would remind him of the absurdity of it to no avail. Before pulling away he would produce a small red 'Silvine' notebook and jot down the exact mileage. He would review the figures in idle moments and later do long-hand maths to arrive at the golden calculation – how many miles the car had done to a gallon on any given journey. With a boyish expression of pleasure he would announce that 'the old girl' was in top form. I assumed he meant his gleaming, black MG which I lovingly polished once a month for extra pocket money.

Over the last few months I noticed that whenever I would recount some anecdote of family life he would permit a wry smile of acknowledgement but would rarely expand.

Was it the effort required to convert memory into speech, I wondered, or simply mental shorthand made audible? I sensed that language was becoming a battleground and that he was not on the winning side. There was an urgency for me to communicate as I knew the art might soon be lost. There were things I wanted to share with him, some intimate things which I had wondered for years if he had ever wondered about.

For all the Christian foundations he had laid and the father-and-son 'talky times' he initiated – which had raised my hopes - there remained events and subjects which I could never explore with him. Maybe if I had persevered I could have led him into uncharted waters... too late for that now. The fact is those times were more like father-to-son where he wanted to confide something of himself, pass on some wisdom on life by virtue of hindsight or about Mum who seemed perpetually unwell. Although the details were often sketchy he was keen to flag up short cuts which he hoped would prevent me taking the long way round.

But youth is impatient with history, and I regret to say that much of his advice has gone unheeded. With plenty of water under my own bridge I realise that wisdom is not genetic, that history will largely repeat itself in each generation. But I am thankful he kept on trying. Truth, he would say, is like a lifeboat: it will always seek to surface.

Dad was an only child, essentially private and self-contained in many ways, something of a loner I suppose. This natural shyness seemed to be at odds with the nature of his chosen path – a twenty-four/seven job, a wide pastoral ministry, an obligation to manage local church politics with periodic accountability to Anglican hierarchy.

The 'alone' parts of his life were his devotions, studying for endless qualifications, sermon preparation and planning for student lectures. He was invariably up at five each morning to spent two hours with God before day started for the rest of the house.

Then I thought about his roots, where his character traits came from. His parents were quiet people, generous, intentional, stubborn and emotionally reserved. I seemed to stay with them often – sometimes days and sometimes weeks – while Mum was in hospital, but I didn't mind; I enjoyed being spoilt. Grandad was a vicar who had a full head of silvery white hair satinized by Brylcreem, and he would fill in for other vicars on holiday or when a local church had no vicar at all. That meant he had to do something called 'crem duty' where I would often accompany him to a local Sussex burial ground and wait in the car with a book while he took a service of departure. As soon as he was out of sight I would take the sumptuous driver's seat, press the pedals, move the stick and turn the wheel making alternate growling and screeching noises – I was desperate to learn to drive. Finally at seventeen he let me use his car and on my first outing along Eastbourne seafront managed to shunt a new Cortina, obviously made of tin foil. Once he showed me the furnace underneath the chapel, and I wondered why they had to burn the box as well as the body. I'm still not sure – perhaps it's for Health and Safety reasons.

I loved the limousines all gleaming black with mirrored chrome, silently obedient with multiple doors, luxurious messengers of death leaving a wake of tragedy and tears. It didn't seem right that ordinary people should have to wait all their lives to ride in the back of a posh estate car all to themselves and not even be conscious of it.

Nanny would address equally earthy matters by admonishing me against the habit of wiping my nose upwards on my handkerchief. She said that it would turn up at the end one day. She was right. I told my Dad and he laughed, remarking that rather than chiding me she should have been happy I had progressed from using my sleeve.

I took the opportunity to say some of the things I felt were important, and I just kept on talking. As this was likely to be the last long journey we would make, it had to be a meaningful one.

Occasionally he used to speak about the place where he and Mum carried out their clandestine courting. Mum was a student at the Royal College of Music when they met and her father had high hopes for her as a concert pianist and viola player. When coaxed she would tell me her own story of playing in the orchestra pit under the direction of Sir Malcolm Sargent, and of course her viola hero was Jacqueline Dupres – a tragic death and so young too. Meanwhile Dad was at Bible College training for the ministry at a time when clergy wives were obliged to sacrifice their vocation in favour of their husband's. Grandad however was determined to prevent this particular union by outlawing it and, as is often the way, encouraged their relationship to blossom. I was happy they met in disobedience.

The lovebirds would travel independently to Hampton Court to hold hands over their favourite river. They dreamed of dining at the adjacent Mitre Hotel – a pot of tea for two with a selection of cakes on the terrace would have been paradise – but they never crossed the threshold. I gave them the opportunity many years later when they came up for their fiftieth wedding anniversary but Dad declined after staring in disbelief at the menu prices. I was proposing to pay for lunch, but he refused to let me waste my hard-earned money! That was my Dad. Suddenly I wished I had insisted.

The light was fading as I stopped the car on the bridge. The easiest thing to do was to carry him from his seat, across the pavement onto a wide stone wall. Checking there were no passers-by I eased him towards the edge. I held him tight and told him I would miss him; that he had done more for me than he could know. I regretted any distance between us geographically and emotionally and that despite the times we were out of joint I loved him deeply. As the moon appeared from behind a silvery cloud, I said, "Goodnight," and I let him fall.

He hit the water and the heavy ashes echoed in the arch of the bridge while the smokey dust was whipped away by a magical evening breeze.

Alex Mowbray

Journey

Infrequent Flyer

I'd forgotten just how long it took
to ready for the trip,
to not forget my books and get a grip on what I can
and cannot pack,
remembering that once upon that plane
there is no going back.

We are most privileged of all the travellers of time
who watch our world shrink down below
while cruising at an altitude
beyond the dreams of those who only knew
a slower way to go.

Essentially a metal tube at speed
with wings to balance and two engines to convey –
we are a miracle defying gravity
and buffeted by turbulence
in pockets of resistance
smug in silent glide.
Enjoy the ride!
Skim heaven just above the clouds
where many suns still shine and peace unbroken reigns,
where nature in its elemental fierceness
refuses to be tamed.
We take our chance
as in our engineering skill advance -
there's something fragile here -
perched on currents up at thirty thousand feet
clinging to the limits of our finite mind.

Alex Mowbray

I stare into infinity and ask
if this is all there is -
more stars and endless space
and long gone vapour trails that traced the journey's end,
that after days and blessed light
eternal night?

A Human, Being

There are times in my life
that if I joined them up
would almost make a season of reflection
resting from the business of the day;
miscellaneous minutes
snatched from the expectations of others, duty bound
or driven by far-reaching guilt,
forever running to catch up;
a bar that's set so high by them
or me:
I could so I should and I really ought to,
you know.
Have I become a human doing?

I want to steal time,
to pinch the second hand,
suspend myself in irresponsibility
and wander freely in the garden of my thoughts
to pause,
reflect on why I'm here
or there
or anywhere.
I just want time to be
in time that's just for me.

Alex Mowbray

Resistance

I am not one who crumples in despair,
wishing the remaining days away
and hating the dark night.
I will fight passivity, frustrated anger and
petulant self-pity.
I will wedge my foot against the door of fate
and thrash the tidal water back and
strain my eyes through shrouding mist
where reason rises up and screams.
Knocked down repeatedly by force of origin unknown
I must get up.
I will get up.

Dream On

When we were young
we'd move so easily from truth to fiction,
tangible to magical,
and by our rich imaginings
the power of make-believe
would infiltrate our thoughts
to turn what was
into our wanting it to be.
Play was what we did
in open season,
timeless freedoms to explore,
no need for reason's boundary
or constraint of common sense.
Dreams flooded in
like running tides o'er shingle sprawl
and then recede with promise to return
at nature's call.
What fun! What happiness!
Boundless in our energy
we ran and climbed
and skipped and tripped
and dressed in costumes we had made
then slept and schemed
another escapade.

Now wiser, older and more sensible,
determined by responsibility,
facing disciplines and fact
we quietly cling to hopes and dreams
however unattainable.
And why is that?
Perhaps we seek escape in fantasy
to turn what is
into our wanting it to be.

Alex Mowbray

Maybe we live through others we know well
ignoring that which stares us in the face
or crave an anaesthetic for the daily pain
so common to the human race.

What's wrong with dreams and longings
when they come?
They're part of who we are,
the child in each of us,
the need to play,
recapturing those care-less worlds
where we would dearly like to stay.
But more than that
they indicate a deeper need -
a foetal need for safety and security,
a kind of voluntary powerlessness
that finds fulfilment through implicit trust.

To know that I am loved
above all human promises,
unkeepable or never meant,
no hurtful arrows ever sent
and tears from such deep joy
with peace that's like pure energy –
is all this possible?
My God has staked his life on it
through Christ our Lord.

The Bridge

Between the cliffs on which we stand
proud, sheer, soaring,
a bridge of sorrows spans our isolation.
Dreams in pieces,
echo of promises now faint,
weary and sick of silence
we contemplate getting in touch again
in a driven sort of way.

By middle-meeting
we resolve to speak the truth -
we know it's going to hurt but
faced with facts and allocated blame
we're done pretending.

Recalling love's first flush,
we miss togetherness when we would rush
to reach the parkland seat
and share the precious moments
of companionship…

Alex Mowbray

The Tongue

The tongue
a blade
a double edge
to bless,
to raise us up
or curse
and cut us down,
to turn a smile
into a frown.
The tongue
untameable,
so unpredictable,
so frighteningly
free.

This Present Age

Some things in life
you notice by their absence -
plants that used to flower
or common courtesy,
trust that gradually evaporates -
in different ways they leave you sad.
What makes you sad?
For many it is fear of growing old,
acknowledging they may not see as they have seen –
it's sobering,
it concentrates the mind.
The days of reasoning, of personal intent are limited;
the time will come when others make key choices in your life.

What can you do?
Evaluate, re-visit dreams,
make each day count
and strengthen what remains.
If time is of the essence choose
what really matters,
letting go of what you will not need
and seek the company of friends
who speak of purpose,
freedom from all fears
who's certainty of hope
can wipe away the tears.

Alex Mowbray

Words of Life

Express the inexpressible!
Rise above the very words you choose!
Make them hang around a while
like mist in early morn.
Deep in your transient dreams
you stub your toe on time, on flesh, on memory.
Young once you jumped and jumped
to grab that branch just out of reach;
now higher still –
you wish that you could fly.
As one would lance a boil
to let the venom out
you've aired your angst on captive ears,
traded on most common fears and
slowly, slowly earned respect.
With tension, power, intensity
you spread your words upon a page,
the evidence of what's inside,
the marks that prove you are alive -
there's something driven isn't there?
Passion in the core of who you are
runs deep beneath the cynic's jibe
– new shoots from our contaminated soil;
the hope that springs
and rushes like the roaring tide
with boundless energy returns
to sprawl upon the beach.
There is a joy unfettered, free,
a celebration of humanity
that used to impact you and me –
is there something that we've missed,
something overlooked, dismissed
or unaccounted for
that whispers why?

Stigma? What Stigma?

You have to look to find it here;
it might be on your street
hidden
for the sake of other people's fear.
Most of us don't really know,
we'd rather not,
one of life's unpleasant facts.
Of course we've heard things,
seen a documentary
but never had to face them in the flesh.
What would we do?
Is there protocol, you know, procedures,
guidelines for our interaction – after all
it's good to be prepared.
Dare we shake a naked hand?
How about a hug, a kiss?
From what we've heard
it's safer just to give the intimate a miss.
Apparently you carry HIV for years
suppressed by drugs and counselling
until your energy runs out
but when your skin erupts in boils and sores -
you just can't hide it anymore.

Full-blown AIDS:
what prejudice in those few words:
not just the devastation or the pain,
the anguish and relentless symptoms –
it's the isolation, separation,
the increasing powerlessness.
What does one say?
'I'm sorry' sounds inadequate.
You ask them how they're feeling and they ask you
if you really want to know.

Alex Mowbray

You don't.
You do.
You're curious –
a person just like you is hosting killer bugs in healthy cells
that gain complete immunity –
ironic isn't it?
You wish them all the best of course
avoiding platitudes while thanking God
you're not like one of them.
They would get out more if they could,
out of their bodies, trade them in
for anything but tortuous departure
of their colleagues and their friends.
Gathered family with brave and desperate eyes
try not to cry.

Being human seems to mean we look for fault,
someone to blame.
Not that we cast first stone
but on the other hand
we're asking questions silently –
shared needles, drugs or dodgy sex perhaps?
Does judgment ration sympathy?
They read your face,
who's side you're on
after you've gone
leaving them alone.
Always alone.
Sometimes though the truth gets out
over the fence or through the school's gate –
respected to rejected in the whisper of a word.
Their kids ignored,
the looks and look-aways,
anger sprayed on windows,

Unquiet Energy

faeces through the letter box
and long, long uncertain days.
At least it's better here than over there
in Africa
where stigma bites deeper than mosquitoes,
where your secret's never safe for long,
where when you lose your job
you'll never get another one,
where treatment is available for some,
where sickness has no Benefit,
where death brings orphans, hardship and
a badge of family shame.
The more sick you are the further the clinic,
the more stories you hear the more they are tragic;
where those in communities who struggle to cope
are deprived of their rights, of their voice, of their hope.
For a woman it's worse – obliged to carry the blame
for man's misdemeanors or a life on the game
and there's plenty out there who love to play God
with dispassionate dogma and judgmental tone
preaching punishment now for sins in the flesh
with a justified sentence of death.
It's the rumours and the whispering,
the tumours and the blistering
that make them feel so apart, so unclean;
infected,
detected,
inspected like a leper
languishing…

What do we care?
We're over here not over there.

Alex Mowbray

Have I Got News for You

Have I told you lately
that I'm anxious,
fearful for your children and the fighting in the streets?
I sense a gathering storm
that will engulf us all in something vast and supernatural.
Jim won't fix this
nor will human government decide the outcome of the battle for the soul.

Suppose there is a way to set our spirits free
by Act of God, Creator of the universe
at whose hand nations rise and fall
who knows us inside out,
the breath we take,
the word that's on our tongue,
the motive of each heart,
our joy, our tears, decisions that we make.

Have I told you lately that we're running out of time,
that those who know must warn the ones who don't;
to pray for Spirit eyes to pierce invisibility
that He who wakes the dead
will shine upon the blind
to warm cold hearts
that all may know an everlasting peace…

Passed Over

I refuse to live in the past
with cling-on memories that cause me
to look over my shoulder
at how things might have been
and being bound by them
limit my usefulness to God.
I reject the world's assessment that I'm spent,
my tank is empty and I'm all but dry.
What is it about age
that generates such stigma,
stares and look-away?
Perhaps others see themselves
and fear the likely days of impotence with rage -
they don't know me
and passing over choose the youth of inexperience.
Like fruit best ripens on the tree,
like seasoned timber soaks up nature's tears
there's value in maturity.
That God invests his time in years is good enough for me.

Alex Mowbray

Man

Image bearer
made in likeness of a holy being
crown of creation unbroken in relationship
who from the garden barred lost Eden's bliss
has walked in darkness ever since
searching for why

Tamer of nature
subjugator of the earth and master of the seas and skies
determines to succeed
omnipotent in his own eyes

What makes a grown man weep
fall on his knees in impotence?
That place where soul to spirit yields
where sunlight's shaft strikes steel
to sever fetters of his sin
to raise horizon eyes and let divine light in

There's beauty here
there's beauty everywhere despite the ugliness of pain
the sun that warms your back
the work that sweats your brow
the desperate need to find a meaning in the things we do…

That we are here today is no coincidence
we walk this journey once
we write our own CV
we strive to make a lasting mark
we leave a legacy

Unquiet Energy

So from conviction's place let hearts be glad!
Let's raise our faith
and seek a closer walk
determined by God's grace to put his kingdom first
that it will temper everything we do –
there is a smile upon His face…

Alex Mowbray

Beauty

Sprung

Growing, going for it,
roots that shoot,
tight buds yield floods of magnificent hues –
spring is absolutely here!
Brand new life from winter's mulch -
those damp and sombre days
have disappeared.
The ruminating bulbs push up,
announce their presence
with a scent so heavenly
as leaves unfold,
stretching sinews to the sun
and waving in a warm and gentle breeze
with vibrant colour, edges crisp;
each plant and bush and tree
clamours in strong silence
to be recognised by me.

Alex Mowbray

Restless Energy

For me the sweetest days
are spring and summer's overlap
when carefree smiles appear
and colour saturates us all;
resonant calls in leafy glades,
fresh meadows tempt the rabbits out
in broad day light.
Everywhere you look there's
flowers that clamour to be seen,
bushes fit to burst,
intrinsic harmony.
In all this magic stillness
there is restless energy.

Contentment

What is it about a garden
slightly wild but not unkempt
and packed with vibrant flowers,
untidy borders that conceal a path,
lush leaves in summer's sun,
those scented evenings breezy, languishing,
so rich in muted colours as the dusk descends?
Is it the being there?
Is it the experience that no-one can destroy?
Perhaps it's the power of nature's gift,
the providence of God,
his common grace to those of faith
and those of doubt
who may not know what life's about
but rest awhile upon the grass
allowing precious time to pass
and find contentment here…

Alex Mowbray

Sounds like Summer

In summer sunshine if they could
the flowers would shout
and buds burst into song,
tight leaves uncurl and stretch
and hum in vibrancy;
the waving grass would shriek
so happy to be free
but actually what happens is
they celebrate quite noiselessly.

Harlyn

Inhaling the breeze, a fresh south-westerly
invigorating senses and my skin
I stand expectant on the damp and springy turf unkempt
and with affectionate eye allow excitement of those
family holidays to flood this bay again.
Boundary rocks rise up matt black, jagged,
rough-hewn by time and a relentless tide
boast mustard lichen clinging in the early light.
Silvery sands deserted save for strollers like myself
await invasion of the day when pleasure seekers revel
in a Cornish paradise.
Breakfast done those eager visitors will stream across
soft ground, a multitude of happy people poised to greet
the roar of rollers racing up the beach.
Catch it! Catch that wave or tumble in the passing surf.
Thrust out those boards, kick hard to feel the thrill!

Me, I'm happy just to stand in awe of ocean's energy,
how it impacts on the land,
how it captivates me every time.

Alex Mowbray

Seagulls

Wheeling seagulls
shrieking at me,
no ties that bind,
no history,
just freedom, sharp-eyed,
such aggressive grace
fierce-fighting over my unfinished chips.

Time and Tide

Soft roar and silky foam greet me on the stone steps
scoured by scores of lapping tides.
I sit down under a silvered moon that tinges raked clouds
in darker ghostliness
while ocean's swell rolls in with unquiet energy so deep,
unfathomable

Many have sat here before yet I, so recently
respect this shore
and re-appreciate cloaked beauty
while the cooler breezes drift on up the beach.
This lack of light that by reducing sight awakens other senses
and restores the thrill of being here;
to let time slide
and with such deep in-filling
takes away my fear

Alex Mowbray

A Sense of the Sea

I love the dawn mist
when the sea breathes
and the shore shivers in anticipation of the day.
Soft sand
pitted by countless feet
yields to the lapping of an early tide
ahead of garrulous gulls in ceaseless search for scraps.
I sense the salt
cleansing, healing, carried by the moon
till waves break free upon the beach.
Expectant walkers feel the first-light chill,
their dogs run heedless in the gentle surf
and peace is pierced.
Horizon blurs where sky and sea discreetly kiss
and distance matters little in this haze…

Summer Slipping

Summer's slipping:
golden curls are seen among the trees.
Breathe in the merest hint of chill
foreshadowing a shorter day
when leaves all bronzed or rusty red
will flutter in such silent grace and
settle gently in the mist
while calls of birds are muted
sensing something.
Damp saturates and bracken
turning brown til spring
defends with dewy fronds young rabbits, mice
against the hov'ring wing

Alex Mowbray

Leaving

Mute golds, soft coppery tints give hint of winter's shift;
summer such as it was is leaving swift as swallows on the wing.
Sensing chill
we contemplate the heating or another layer at least
but pause in disbelief.
So soon our morning breath suspending,
pending a different time of year…
Grass gives up its dew,
gardens not so formal now with petals softly falling
stained with autumn rust;
another month and blustery winds among the trees
will ease them of their load
littering the park, the path, the road.

Nature embraces change so painlessly.

Fall

Red, yellow, bronze and brittle brown,
the leaves are set to fall fluttering
on to grass still green -
the rot has set in.
Curling, damp and blown around
then herded into heaps by blustery wind
the summer coverings decay
enriching soil that feeds the root of spring.

Alex Mowbray

Mist and Mystery

Enigmatic light invades the chill air, bright
with deep deceptive shadows rich in tone
and heavy with the scent of rottenness;
my cloudy breath hangs for a few seconds
as I stand upon the river's bank
in dewy undergrowth.
It's wonderful to be alive, here
where the river gently curves
and disappears in mist and mystery,
deeply breathing fresh moist air
and wishing I could hold this moment,
take it captive, take it home…

Park Life

So clear this morning, bright and sharp,
as summer's generous greenery bows to
red rust, gold
and gentle fallings.
So soon it seems
those soft and floaty days,
lazy and luxuriant,
give way to dark, stark shapes against a thin, cold sky.

Majestic in decay, these leaves of life
litter my park.
I'm early at the gates and first to tread the carpet
crisp with frozen dew.
But where to now?
The hill I know so well or somewhere new?
I love the landscaped gardens way beyond the wood;
where secret gardeners hoe and prune,
tidy twigs and keep the hedgerows neat.
I like to sit on wooden seats that Rest In Peace and gaze
on beds of multicoloured blooms. Those beds,
now empty save for winter's mulch, are slightly warm and
yield a different kind of sweetness to the air.

Skinny shadows laying long on frosted grass, broken
over tufty hummocks rising from unkempt terrain and
in the mist of distance
grey-green fences guard a magic place…

As I swing the newly-treated gate
a squirrel stops, stares, then scampers up the nearest trunk;
a rustle just a bush away and crackling twigs remind me
I am not alone.
I walk with cloudy breath, my senses bristling
at covert scampering along the ground.

Alex Mowbray

I've reached black-water pond with brittle skin
and pointy reeds that stand so tall
all matt and velvety.
Am I the master here?
I felled a tree, I built a bridge and re-diverted streams;
I am the architect of this plot's grander scheme
but crouching still beside the pond
I feel the spirit of the earth.
I smile at what is going on beneath my feet,
above my head,
the creep and crawl,
the flutter and the flap,
organic harmony.

Perhaps my role is nature's nurturer to raise
what has been born;
the steward of a deeper mystery
who revels in a brand new dawn...

Season Greetings

a wealth of concentrated smells from boggy undergrowth
steeped in driven rain refresh me once again

resonant bellows of a rutting stag dull-echo in the mist

raked leaves await their fate as winter's mulching beckons –
preparation's underway

conkers litter chestnut trees so free for foragers
and dew weeps everywhere

colours intensify
rich hues
in dying bursts
bowing to a chill wind

Alex Mowbray

Fallen

Pitted yellow, brittle bronze and
rich in rotteness
the lifeless leaves lay damp, dishevelled,
homeless in a heap;
brisk sweep - now all their glory's gone.
Bare branches sway in bitter wind
and yearn for spring
whose buds will overcome all winter's weariness.

Winter's White

Stark
branches
greyish green
laden with winter's white
overhang slip-slidey pavements;
determined traffic struggles up the road
acknowledging the power of frozen rain to paralyse
and lay to waste, so beautifully indifferent to our plight.
Overnight the fresh flakes fall to settle on an icy undertow;
amid the beauty it is treacherous, shutting in the timid and the frail,
disrupting working days and disappointing travellers but even so there's
something
magical…

Alex Mowbray

Mortality

News at Ten

Hardly a day goes by
without mention of a tragedy
in tones reserved for heroes,
sentences sustained
with sombre face, eyebrows slightly drawn.
You leap ahead – how many dead?
At worst unnumbered souls
who never stood a chance
but hopefully survivors
who last at least til dawn.
It might be ethnic slaughter,
a very nasty accident or
a threat we have ignored.
We sigh with corporate grief
silently frustrated at their sense of loss;
we agonise at others' shock,
their utter helplessness
while we the powerless
rage inwardly at a flat screen.
Death and damage in the midst of life;
terror on the rampage,
a war against the body and the soul.
Technically we are omnipotent
genetically we can manipulate,
so close to choosing who we want
and who we don't.
There's pictures from infinity,
a universe next door,
despite the news from round the world
we cannot
or we will not feed our poor.

Alex Mowbray

Inhuman nature
unenlightened
could destroy itself through lawlessness
and a critical loss of identity.

Endtime

History repeats itself and (hard of hearing)
fails to read the signs.
Unguarded is the blindness of the mind -
war rages on within this inner man
for these are times of desperation not so quiet,
unbridled anger,
child abuse enough to make you weep;
taken life, so cheap, is barely news
and hope can vanish overnight.

What is it sickens us,
that drives anxiety, disgust;
the yearning for those happier days?
Uncertainty.
Deep doubt.
Things out of our control.
Into this the persecuted prophets speak
who dared to raise their voice three thousand years ago
about a dark deception brooding,
chaos in the wings,
the ghost in our machine…

One Name is written in the wind, trustworthy, pure,
the Searcher of all hearts,
who raises bodies from the dead
and reaches out pierced hands to rescue from the mess,
to raise us in redemption's grip
and plant us in God's promised land.

Alex Mowbray

The Guardian

I knew him from somewhere;
a pleasant smile and courteous.
Wheeled in, a few tables away
I would observe
discreetly
in the sunlit room for visitors.
I could never catch his words;
he came, he chatted reassuringly
to others in the room
and always smiled at me
then disappeared.

I don't remember much about the accident
except the blinding lights,
the impact and the smoke
then nothing til a gentle voice
and faces upside down.
I turned my eyes and blinked
and swallowed hard from thirst
and beckoning with wider eyes
one face came close and smiled
so warm, so wise.
I tried to speak –
she hushed my lips then went
and came with one in white
who sat on mattress edge
and told me plainly what the long words meant..

Those first few weeks were dark
with terrors in the night;
bright lights re-lived
and daily the despairing.
Though I could barely turn my head
they'd prop me up in case of visitors

Unquiet Energy

most breezy bright,
some weary from the trip
and nearly all would pass my feet.
The sallow youth accross the ward looked ill.
He rarely smiled or raised his head;
the food trays passed him by and
curtains often flew around his bed.
His parents would come in,
his Mum all anxious; when they left
I'd see his face so sad, so thin.
His Dad was always smart in dark blue suit;
his gentle smile acknowledged nursing staff –
he seemed to notice everyone
and always smiled at me.

One day
they moved me to a residential home
and then fermenting anger rose, turned in
and made me sick that I,
chair-chained by some split-second smash,
would never use my limbs again.
I longed to raise a glass
or scratch an itch,
to wave goodbye or post my friend a card,
to bath myself and grab fresh towels
but as my body had become
I couldn't even move my bowels.
Descending gloom and pity-me
consumed my early thoughts
and six months on still had nose-diving days
with anguished tears of deep frustration
sometimes turning into rage.

Alex Mowbray

Adrift in semi-sleep one afternoon
forced on me by the baking sun
I focussed on the shape in front -
a blue-suit man was crouched and smiling.
He told me that the youth across the ward
had caused the crash that put me here;
that he was not his Dad
and stretching out his hand
he laid it on my head and then my heart
to pray forgiveness in
and while I sobbed quite helplessly
and went to sleep in peace,
he disappeared.

Fatality Flowers

Fatality flowers in stained cellophane
clinging to the railings in the fast lane,
grim reminder to the scarred and the scared
of one so young.
We stand in sadness
in memoriam,
in tangible agony with moist cheeks
and quiet tongue –
what is there to say?
If he'd been really old
or had a heart attack
or even dozed off at the wheel
it would have made more sense
but this,
this is madness by another name
inexplicable to us, heads buried in our grief
and huddled close against life's bitter wind.

Alex Mowbray

Glory Fields

Motionless in the hanging mist
I feel interminable damp
and stinking sodden leather
hell in trenches deep in water
thick in mud
swathes of soldiers scythed like wheat
haphazard in the mire

In all this deathly silence
there is still no peace
as I stand among the empty shells and
soft groans of the unquiet

I clutch my medals to my chest
and see my friends
brothers in arms wasted in no man's land
then fifty years of anger rises at the tragic loss of life
for greater good
for peace in our time

It won't bring Berty back
or Derek
Edward
John
but I can stand here
gazing at dog-eared photos in the freedom they achieved
acknowledging their sacrifice
while glory fields live on

Gone

Her life became a lie
too difficult to live;
she chose to die,
no note.
Whispers at the graveside
bleak with grief –
who knew, who tried?
She left no clue,
she left two children
three and five;
she left without a warning;
she left her mother
wondering...

Alex Mowbray

On Ageing

She glanced
and in the mirror unforgiving
met her mother's eyes.
She thought of mother resting now,
her deeper creases, welcome, warmth,
her openness, her heart of gold,
her stories and her legacy of life,
the wisdom of the old.

Mortality

What is life worth?
I don't mean in body parts
or research specimens,
I mean intrinsic value,
the kind you measure in emotions
the ones you'll really miss,
those you would defend and struggle for
and maybe in so doing
put your life at risk.
For some through human history
it's been about a cause:
justice, freedom, peace,
the right to basically exist,
more recently a greener world,
equality of race.
Dwelling on mortality concentrates the mind.
It's sobering; who's taken, how and when
so I try not to think about it
but time goes by,
the years put creases in my face;
I realise that what I've done
is more than half I'm going to do.
I'm re-evaluating me – what am I worth
but how critique myself? I hear
what others kindly say
and sometimes what they don't.
I want to make a different mark
from those scratched on a prison wall;
I want to leave a trail, a legacy,
something precious, individual,
positive and inspirational,
uniquely me.

Alex Mowbray

Together

"Sixty two years," he cried,
"and it's come to this;"
the anguish in his tears
he could not hide.

Sixty two cards he chose
to express his love;
such deep companionship
that no-one knows.

Bed-bound he grasped my hands
and red anger rose
then sobbed in helplessness
with no demands

So ill, she came to him
but he couldn't speak
for shame and pale despair
of eyes grown dim.

Coming of Age

My father, stick in hand
answered the door.
His cheery smile creased pleasant lines,
warm handshake and a hug
welcomed the prodigal.
Shorter I thought
with noticeable stoop - brief shock -
for he and I were six foot tall for years.
At eighty five he's looking good;
the dog is walked, the shopping's done
and in between his frequent sleeps
there's constant care for Mum
who isn't well.
Her body seems to fight itself
compounded by frustrations of an active mind
with bones that crumble
and a stick to compensate
for doctors who don't seem to care.

I understand the problem started
when she'd given birth to me;
I don't know why, I haven't asked
for fear I triggered her malaise.
Faint resonance of guilt
each time I hear
about the latest agony
and disappointment medically
and can't move this
and daren't lift that
and Dad, if he fell over
well, what would she do?
No blame.
If only I 'lived nearer, love'.
We've all made choices;

Alex Mowbray

independence
is a powerful force,
defines our distances
in miles and memories
and practicalities of care.

They're going to move.
Again? They're going to move
whenever trauma threatens their mobility
at least three times a year.
They're going to stay;
they'll manage,
they'll get someone in,
they like this house too much
and anyway the operation's booked –
was that the shoulder or the hip?
I offer my advice
that one day choice will be a luxury
and others may determine where they go.
How wise, how thoughtful, yes I'm right,
they'll have another think.

Sofa photos document events
and placing them in time we tell
their stories, who was there
and who has gone.
Happy memories
coming out to play,
unique to us as family
are precious and
significant.
Tears trickled too,
brief,
wincing over scars of pain

Unquiet Energy

from sickness
and the languishing.

Time for tea.
Crustless sandwiches so neatly cut
decorate the Minton plates
all cling film wrapped,
with salted peanuts, walnut cake
and fine bone china cups.
The kitchen shuffle at an end
Mum has hers in her chair
but will Dad sit with me?
A deeply private only child
deflecting questions
which invite him to reveal.
I should behave myself,
it's just that I don't really know
this man who fathered me.

Alex Mowbray

Circles

I didn't want it to be this way.
I have more thinking time
now that arthritis has set in.
I hate being an inconvenience
(they insist that I'm not);
I know I cramp their style
(although they never breathe a word);
apparently I am fragile these days
(the children have been told to keep the noise down).
I am seventy two years young today
and as I watch excited faces approach me for a hug
joy surges from my heart and I break out in smiles
of dreams fulfilled;
disparity of years is vanquished by a sweet embrace.
Without me this couldn't happen,
without my input they would not be here;
the circle is complete and meaning lies herein
with such deep joy!
What floods my soul with peace and sweetness
is impossible to say;
I wouldn't have it any other way.

Doorways

So slow it seems is death's ensuing sleep,
so painful for the friends who wait and weep
in anguish at the bitterness of memories so sweet:
why does it have to be this way?
We want a softer place, an in-between
where angels keep the door of death ajar,
where spirits move to comfort us, the left behind
and somehow make it easier.
Oh dear departed
smug in your silence like the mountain mist,
deaf to bereavement's cry,
involuntary tears at intimacies shared
and all our emptiness; we know
we are appointed once to die.

Alex Mowbray

My Dad, Late On

Eight stone and a shadow of a man –
his eyes are closed;
he hasn't seen me at the door frame of the ward.
He is so still; is he asleep? Did I arrive too late?
Suddenly I saw him in a padded box face up
serene, retouched for relatives.
'Not yet, not yet' the boy inside me cried
and as I move towards the bed
an eyelid flickers into life –
he slowly turns his head to catch my smiling face.
His eyes are misty blue, familiar
for in my younger days they pierced me
in the search for truth, those kind blue eyes
to match a servant heart.
Pulling up a chair I kiss his head
and as he takes my hand I see the thinly printed gown
fall lightly off his shoulder to reveal
a shocking skinniness.
Is this the strong broad-shouldered man
who stood in Reverend authority
a full two inches taller than myself?
Where that sonorous pulpit voice
that held me with a mix of fear and grace
for thirty minutes twice a week?
Where too the grip of welcome out of joy
and deep unspoken gratitude?
They are all here
hinted in his wan complexion,
pathetic frailty and those eyes.
He looks hard at me in helplessness,
dependence and increasing weariness.
Still clinging to my hand and quality of life
we chat with spaces, 'How is Mum?
Good to see you; family alright?'

Unquiet Energy

'You have to eat more Dad,
you won't stand up on soup and custard -
please co-operate.'
He knows. He'll try, it's very difficult,
he hates this place, confusion's setting in.
I sense a kind of ghostly-ness
as if the inner man is letting go,
relinquishing it's grip;
my Dad is moving into peace.

Alex Mowbray

Laters

They tell me you came and sat on the bed;
apparently I never heard a word that you said.
I feel your warm breath on my face,
your soft voice invading my space;
as I drift on through my chemical dream
I sense the ghost in my beeping machine.

I turn over
figures of speech in my mind –
despite eyelids
heavy with lethargy
I will know if you've been
rehearsing hushed tones
and dignified exits
and catch you later
and anything I want?

What I want you cannot give.
What I would trade you would not like.
I have no value now save in your memory.
Will I hear my final breath,
the deepest sigh that shuts the body down?
After, when the plugs are pulled
and relatives have been informed
and so-called friends I haven't seen for years
will gather round my grave to offer tears
will you still sit on my bed
and promise that you'll see me later on?

Sweet Release

Her living it was long,
her dying swift,
thank God.
I think she knew
at a stroke
by frailty,
by pain of fractured frame.
Release was sweet from suffering,
frustrations of an active mind
and wretched immobility.
At peace,
her work is done;
her children's tears recall a cheerful Mum,
her hope for brighter days;
love's legacy.

Alex Mowbray

Spaces

I feel I'm half the man he was
or little more.
I ache.
I miss him.
There are spaces in my day -
the calls I'd make;
that cheery voice without complaint
but weariness of age
and stiffening joints
and routine care for Mum
had slowed him down.

So ill, she came to him
but he couldn't speak
for shame and pale despair
of eyes grown dim.

A Sense of Wonder

I think about you often
wondering
what it was really like
to walk the earth with holy feet,
to greet your neighbours on the street
with God's own heart to feel the beat of all humanity.
Sensing that one day you would be king
and leave behind a loyal band
you understood compassion's pain,
made ready for a traitor's blow
then willingly you let life go...

Alex Mowbray

The Cross Road

There is comfort in the cross –
hard, gnarled
rough-carved and splintering
to match the jagged lives
of those strung out and left to die.
What comfort then?
The one we worship
volunteered his perfect life
and as the chosen lamb
yielded up his majesty
to spear and thorns and soldier's barb
to hang in isolation, agony,
achieving in those final hours
acceptance by creator God;
that all our sin would wash away,
that we could live in him
forever and a day.

One Off

A life returned to sender with a legacy of pain
that bore the burden of our ignorance.
Once and for all,
prophetic call upon his life,
with outstretched arms
he reasoned to reach up
and bring his heaven down
to earth
to heal the blindness of the eye,
the deafness of the ear,
flood peace into the turmoil of the inner man.
We will remember him
whose blood-soaked cross cried innocence,
a strategy beyond his time
whose kingdom's here and now
and will be later on.

Alex Mowbray

Hope

Tick Tock

I watched a short film once
in which time passed
mostly in silence
save the ticking of a clock.
The camera panned the room in lonely monochrome -
alighting on a chair it prompted speech – an old man's voice.

In warm yet wistful tones he recalled memories of joy,
of family and laughter - brightness in the air;
of presents, games and visits to the fair
when chill autumnal nights wrapped darkness all around,
star-struck by the roaring rides,
transfixed by spotlight glare.

He yearned for morning rambles
and the haystack romps at Valley Farm,
rolling and tumbling in harvest's gold and irresponsibility of youth;
reckless skirmishes on brake-less bikes
and cancer sticks shared deep among the shadows of the shed.
Ah, the bliss of ignorance.

He paused;
continuing with melancholic edge
about the fewer, shorter visits now;
the busy lives, the 'sorrys' and the awkward silences;
the gift-wrapped packets through the post
and scribbled foreign cards from grandkids en vacances.

Alex Mowbray

It wasn't lack of love, he thought.
It wasn't that they didn't care.
He reasoned that they'd all grown up,
sprouted wings,
just left him in his chair.

They didn't need him like they did.

Time
calibrated by indifference then
became so measured,
ominous,
marching to a beat.
Segmented silences now generated fear, uncertainty;
the heavy seconds seemed to wrestle with his very soul
and make him ask tough questions, ducked 'til now.

Way back in short-trousered Sunday School
a kind, tall smiling face had reassured him of his Friend in heaven
blended in of course with being good and sitting still,
discouraging the picking of the nose and trying not to cry.
Where was that friend now?
Was He like so many in his later life more word than deed,
oozing with evaporating promises and well intentioned thoughts?
Did He in fact exist at all?
Perhaps like the clock against the wall
He'd wound up tight the spring of nature,
moved on to higher things and left the world to run…

Unquiet Energy

But no.
If He was God, His promise had to be forever. Pondering,
he sensed those early sins foreshadowed future and more serious things –
they'd pointed out his path to heaven's door.
Had he, a mortal coiled in mixed emotion, earned the right to contact
Immortality - risking rejection yet again?

The answer came.
The ticking stopped
and as he called out "Friend" the word died on his lips.

Alex Mowbray

Hopers

Horror on a hill of skulls,
shudder at resounding thuds
through seared flesh into
solid wood blackened,
stained from incarcerated blood,
all knotty, gnarled;
three sharp shapes against a bruising sky
before the pitched dark.
Life at an end,
head hung in agonizing peace
pending a promise,
a prophecy of old foretold
to those who dreamed one day of liberation.
Dying to save,
dying to rise
dying to know the outcome they waited
in an upper room, locked in
in fear
with just the scent of hope...

When Questions Come

Things aren't what they seem
like our slow-rolling world so natural, serene
as seen from out in space;
like those we've known for many years
revealing who they really are;
like what we know of God.
There seems to be a time in everybody's life
when questions come
and answers don't,
when what we think we know is not enough to satisfy
and questioning begins
propelled by sickness or the death of someone near,
relentless reasoning, deep disillusion or a curiosity -
we must know why we're here.
Strangely
the one who only spoke the truth was brutalised;
the perfect man who understood our deepest needs
was left to hang
but
you can't kill God for long.

Alex Mowbray

Morning Glory

The tomb of doom is flooded with a shaft of light.
Had the soldiers still been guarding
they would probably have died of fright.
Who moved the stone?
Unwrapped the bandages?
Oh and where's the body gone?
It makes no sense and then you think
six hundred years before
the prophets told us everything:
you can't kill God for long.
Mary in the garden searching,
clinging to Christ's promises – he would return
but nowhere to be seen.
Now there's the gardener, he's bound to know.
'Have you seen my Lord?'
He answers in familiar tone with just one word
and glory dawns...

Sweet Sorrow

When someone dies
the friends all gather round
a wooden box
remembering how good he was,
how kind;
a better man you would not find.
Imagine he could hear!
Perhaps he'd flush with pride
or wriggle with embarassment.
He might just sit up straight
and ask them why he'd had to wait so long
for all these compliments.
Who would he thank?
Why had they saved them up
like pennies in a piggy bank?

Some quite beside themselves
still question why he had to go
and how unfair it is.
Amid the gracious eulogies
and humour tissue-wrapped,
the sweetness and the bitterness
join reassuring hands.
His friends file slowly out,
heads bowed in reverence
and hope one day to re-unite
in different lands.

Few people want to think
that when you're gone you're gone.
Believing that we'll see them all again
gives greater meaning to this life on earth,
a sense of worth,
our only link with immortality.

Alex Mowbray

What is the basis of this hope -
wishful thinking, a hedge against despair
or refusal to accept that this is all that's there?
Not many have returned
to tell us what it's like.
The one who everybody knows about
they don't believe.
He even prophesied his death
and how he'd go
and told us just how long
before he'd breathe again;
how everyone would know
and those who understood
would celebrate and seek to show
the world about the hope
that is a certainty;
that through a faith in him
we too will die
yet live with him
in sweet eternity.

Where Do We Go From Here?

Jesus Christ
Dismissed as swiftly now as when he walked
in Palestine.
A good man, yes,
a prophet some would say
but Son of God?
Beaten, bruised, bleeding
this Jewish king was offered up
to jagged nails:
the first pierce of the skin
held taught by angry arms so full of hate
and orders from on high
to finish Christ the Roman way.
Relentless thud
thud
the flow of blood;
pain bites, arms still outstretched
embracing those who banished him.
Our all-but-lifeless Lord
left hanging,
weeping,
anguished
and alone;
thorn-crowned for all of us.
How is that good news?
Because he rose again and guaranteed that we could know
a holy God.
The future is secure
for those who put their trust in him.

Alex Mowbray

The invitation is for all
to get in touch with Truth,
to give real meaning to our journey through this world,.
to find out why we're here;
and reassure us in our doubt and fear.
The mirror looked at me today
reflecting back a wrinkled prune.
Despite intensive nightly cream
religiously applied,
eternal youth is but a dream!
As time goes by
the signs of age
remind us where we've been.
Many think that when we're dead we're gone,
that dust returns to dust and insignificance -
no traces left bar memories of mourning friends
and graves to put the flowers on.
Imagine this:
that death is not the end
but only our release from human life
which yields our spirit back to God
who gave it anyway.
We have a choice to make:
believe in someone we can't see,
entrust our heart and soul to him
or live in constant wondering
what lies beyond...
We can know now -
God tells us in His book.
The opportunity is here today –
don't wait for how and why.

Unquiet Energy

What brings you here?
A friend, persuasion, curiosity,
how often you have thought there's more to life than this;
the need for hope or healing
or a tug you really can't explain?
We're all unique –
our shape, our size, our history,
however much we own or earn
or how we see ourselves.
God's love is universal yet
He knows our every need,
what drives us on,
our dreams and hopes
and what the future holds.

By exercising simple faith,
by reaching out to one we cannot see as yet,
acknowledging the error of our ways
and recognising Jesus paid our debt
we will know Truth,
revealed in spirit to our hearts
and guidance day on day.
This knowledge is about relationship.
We have a journey's friend;
our eyes are opened by his light;
He speaks in gentle power.

Where will you go from here?

Alex Mowbray

Purpose

Unquiet Energy

These are the Days

These are days of wobble:
corporate insecurity,
tremors of uncertainty,
damage limitation and insolvency,
survival of the fattest
and houses built on sand.
God help us.
What makes you think he's there at all
and listening,
remotely interested in the mess we're in?
Nature does what nature is;
it's down to us to sort it out.
What happens if we don't
or won't
or can't,
what then?
It's easy to be scared,
to carry fear unspoken, deep,
a kind of dread,
the kind you bury til a headline digs it up.
Yet hope survives
surging to the surface lifeboat-like;
you cannot sink, you have responsibilities,
doesn't everything depend on you?
You've watched your new-born shape your days,
compassion moves you in mysterious ways;
the life-force is so strong.
It gets you out of bed, obliges you to eat,
makes you search for something better
and sift the ashes of defeat.
Desperate for meaning behind the news at ten
you dare to open wide horizon eyes
and in the isolation of an anguished heart
you contemplate a god,

Alex Mowbray

an interactive one
who knows what's going on
who having set things up could never walk away.
He is not far from us
in fact.

Be Still

The searcher of our hearts for faith
would spend more time with us,
a friend for life,
a presence felt.
He'd share his breakfast on the beach
and can our wayward spirits teach;
he loves our company.

What calls upon your day outweigh
the need to stop, be still
and in your intimacy pray
his will be done,
his kingdom come;
to learn that less is more
in God's economy?

All You Need is Love

He loves me
He loves me not
He loves me
He loves me not
He loves me
He loves me not

He loves me.

Our Time [1]

A time to reflect and a time to reject,
A time to recall and a time to forgive,
A time to dismantle and a time to rebuild,
A time to cling on and a time to let go,
A time to be emptied and a time to be filled,
A time to be gentle and a time to be blunt,
A time to give way and a time to stand firm,
A time to be silent and a time to speak out,
A time to party and a time to fast,
A time to lay everything down and let God pick it up

---

[1] Based on Ecclesiastes 3:
"There is a time for everything and a season for every activity under heaven."

Alex Mowbray

In Your Dreams

In your wildest dreams
there's meaning,
an interpretation that makes sense.
Tell it to me,
write it down,
date and title it
for God himself can speak in symbols
and surprise you
where you are
right now.

The God of this World

The deepest form of jealousy drives him to undermine,
to mock, corrupt and make us all look fools.
Our finite minds need more than science on our side
when psychics skulk and prowl,
deceiving many that they know what lay beyond.
But God, our Majesty, has clipped his wings
lest he who flies in face of Truth should rise above the earth
accusing even those whose names are in the Book of Life.

What shall I call him who loves to pick off the weak,
that most contemptible who threatens Kingdom work
and seeks to keep us all in comfortable sleep?
He of numbered days,
the prince of dinginess who loathes the light,
pretender to the Kingly throne,
the power of the air whose purpose is to skew,
to shift the blame;
condemned to writhe and wriggle in the grip of shame.

I will not speak his name.

Alex Mowbray

His Majesty

For we, who have no king
except the one who laid aside his crown,
enthrone him in your hearts today!

Risen and ascended now
Christ sits at God's right hand
and guarantees one day that we
will reign with him through all eternity...

These Days

We have sown seeds for long enough,
waited patiently for God's outpouring power.
We've lifted holy hands by grace and humbly bowed our knees –
how long, O Lord, how long?
Our cry's gone up to rattle Heaven's seeming brass
but still His questions hold:

*"How much do you want all I have in mind for you?.
Remember from convicted will
your founding fathers moved their tents;
adjacent to the river royal
encamped upon a powerful land,
and beacon-like would shine in time -
they've prospered at my hand.
You doubt that all the words you've had in prophecies and dreams
will come to pass?
I pledge to deal in all affairs of men,
who is raised up and how and when
according to my purposes
and I delight in you, my children, here and now!
I love you with an everlasting love
and watch as any parent does those first few faltering steps
yet moving in such confidence –
you've not been here before."*

Embrace the vision, church, with softer, open hearts;
survey the landscape of your life and, rich in expectation, take a risk
where hope is based on certainty
and doubt a stepping stone to faith;
there's so much more!
This is our promised land…

Alex Mowbray

Changing

We are not the same as we were
we have grown up
older
wiser hopefully
we are further on in our journey.
Looking back
what do we find
what highlights/lowlights come to mind?

Do we know God better?
Oh we've learnt more about him
but is he now our friend?
When he walks and talks with us
like on Emmaus Road
what does he say?
Does he hang his head in his hands
grief-like
and weep for what is lost
or does he ask a question:
"Do you want all I have for you?"
"I came that your joy could be full
and flowing over in the spirit of the gifts.
I died so you might all have life
and tell the world and break the power of night
discerning Satan's grip
releasing and reclaiming in the truth of light
to raise the roof in praise
and glorify my name."
Jesus
Jesus
there is no other name
Empty and waiting to be filled
to be refreshed
we wait

Unquiet Energy

in expectation meet
like children at your feet
we need you more than ever now.
Lord search our hearts and
Spirit pour in what we need to hear.
We will not fear for you have chosen us
to carry hope and freedom
to a waiting world…

Alex Mowbray

Similar Books by the Publisher

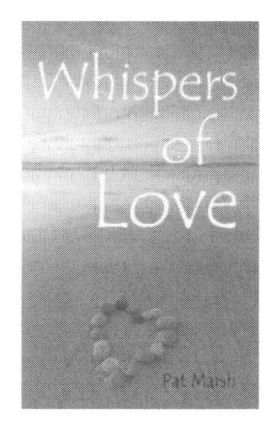

Whispers of Love
Pat Marsh

Chronicling a journey of faith, from its hesitant beginnings to an assurance of being deeply loved, this reprint of Pat Marsh's best-selling anthology is as fresh and engaging today as when it first appeared in print. This collection of simple meditations is a rich resource for reflection, worship and personal prayer.

Pat Marsh is an internationally known writer and retreat leader who has won many awards and is also the author of two other books.

Recycled
Ann First

Ann firth expresses in her poetry how her life was completely 'recycled' by an encounter with God in her later years. When she allowed him to take over her life in 1980 she began to see Him open a whole new life before her.

Through a prophetic word she began writing poetry in 2006 and was able to express, through her poems, how God brought her through some of the difficult times of her life. The book is an opportunity for her to share those times with a wider audience and to encourage others to allow God to recycle them too.

Released
Robert Miller

Robert Miller found the greatest prize of all when he found himself in prison. His poems represent the emotions and gratitude of finding real freedom - a freedom that can never be taken away.

Released is a collection of his writings, both in prison and when released.

Books Available From
www.onwardsandupwards.org